ARCHITECTURE
OF ROME

ARCHITECTURE OF
ROME

A NINETEENTH-CENTURY
ITINERARY BY

Giovanni Battista Cipriani

INTRODUCTION BY
Stanley Tigerman

Sepolcro di S. Vibio Mariano

RIZZOLI

NEW YORK · 1986

Published in the United States of America in 1986 by
Rizzoli International Publications, Inc.
597 Fifth Avenue, New York, NY 10017

Copyright © 1986 Rizzoli International Publications, Inc.

LIBRARY OF CONGRESS
CATALOGING-IN-PUBLICATION DATA

Cipriani, Giovanni Battista, b. 1776.
Architecture of Rome.

Captions to the plates in Italian.
Originally published under title: Itinerario
figurato degli edifici più rimarchevoli di Roma.
1. Architecture—Italy—Rome—Guide-books.
2. Rome (Italy)—Antiquities—Guide-books.
3. Italy—Antiquities—Guide-books. 4. Rome
(Italy)—Description—Guide-books. I. Tigerman,
Stanley, 1930–   . II. Title.
NA1120.C6213   1987   720'.945'632   86–25992
ISBN 0–8478–0776–2

Printed and bound in the United States of America

INTRODUCTION

Giovanni Battista Cipriani published his *Itinerario figurato degli edifici più rimarchevoli di Roma* between 1835 and 1837. This superb collection of 100 plates contains a total of 730 drawings that document elevations, sections, floor plans, and site plans of ancient monuments, churches, bridges, fountains, and public and private buildings of architectural significance—essentially all that was consequential of the Rome of his time. Of course, much of the architectural detail Cipriani depicted has eroded with time, but that does not take away from the stunning precision of the drawings. Indeed, in a few cases, the monuments shown here no longer exist: even the citizens of Rome have, on occasion, suffered a lapse of preservation consciousness.

Example: S. Giacomo Scossacavelli (pl. 95), located between the Borgo Novo and Borgo Vecchio, was demolished during Benito Mussolini's regime to clear the site for an expanded via della Conciliazione in order to extend the axis of S. Pietro to the Tiber River.

Example: S. M. della Sanità (pl. 48), and S. Paolo P. Eremita (presumably by Clemente Orlandi) (pl. 48), were apparently demolished to clear the site for the Ministero dell' Interno on the Quattro Fontane.

Example: Casa di Raffaello (pl. 68), originally thought to have been designed by Bramante.

Nevertheless, even today Cipriani's little book serves as an excellent guide to the Eternal City in many ways. Not least of these are his provision of the name of the architect, where possible, and the date of the work's construction. But certainly the most useful feature of this guide is the visual presentation of each work. For the provision of orthographic drawings rather than the more picturesque and typical *veduti* marks this document as an architectural one. Cipriani's guidebook gives us Rome through the eyes, hand, and mind of a nineteenth-century Italian architect.

Did Signor Cipriani publish all these images—drawn by himself and other architects—primarily for his own edification and that of others of his profession? It would seem so, as a lay audience would probably have had difficulty reading the abstract language of architectural drawing. This observation suggests that the guidebook was intended not for popular tour-taking through the Eternal City, but for purposes of professional study and analysis. Further evidence of this is the fact that significant dimensions are given for each built work. This information in a curious way lifts the architecture out of its historical context and gives it something of the immediacy of the working drawing. Likewise, by refusing to embellish the drawings or 'render' them three-dimensional through conventional techniques, and by describing the buildings in a form hypothetically like that in which the original authors conceived their work, Cipriani creates a bond between architect and trained viewer, designer and a future generation of designers. This 'time warp,' preserving and projecting the original architectural conception, gives the buildings a presence and a life beyond that which could have been suggested by more literal, three-dimensional representationalism. It also marks this work as something to be studied: casually or in detail, as the reader wishes.

Nonetheless, the interest of Cipriani's document extends far beyond that of professionals intent on scrutinizing drawings in order to discover architectural precedents. The connoisseur of drawings and etchings of any era will find this compact recording of the Rome of a bygone era sufficiently absorbing to command his attention while comfortably ensconced in an armchair far from the city that this work marks and measures.

*   *   *

A useful little book, this one. Disarmingly straightforward, it contains much that is of interest to contemporary architects of both amateur and professional stripe. As long as architects continue to journey to Rome in order to measure, draw, and reconstruct the ancient monuments as well as the buildings of the Renaissance, Mannerist, and Baroque epochs, this guidebook will be a valuable companion. And the casual tourist, too, may now possess information only available otherwise in textbooks of architectural history.

In my many travels to Rome, I always yearned for a compact guide to the many monuments of this city with the greatest density of architecture of any in the world. In fact, my desire was to carry with me two portable volumes—one full and one empty: the first, a small, lucid guidebook brimming with architectural information such as contained in the one here; the second, a fresh sketchbook, waiting to be filled with vignettes and ideas inspired by this magical city. I browsed for years in antiquarian bookstores in Rome and abroad before finding the present book. Then, by accident of course, in the spring of 1985 I finally came across it. Here it is in facsimile: this marvelous little book composed of wonderfully artless, perfectly readable etchings of the Rome of another time—indeed, of all time.

STANLEY TIGERMAN

Chicago, August 1986

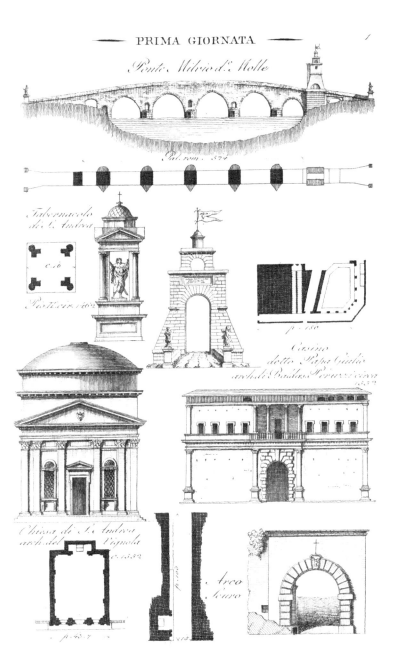

Ponte Milvio d.º Molle

Pal. rom. 324

Tabernacolo
di S. Andrea

c.16

Post Kcir. 1465

Casino
detto Papa Giulio
arch. di Baldass. Peruzzi circa
1552

p. 180

Chiesa di S. Andrea
arch. del   Vignola
c. 1552

p. 43.7

Arco
Scuro

p. 105

v.15

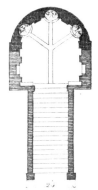

*Fonte
dell' acqua acetosa
Arch. del Bernini
1662*

Casino di Giulio III. Arch. del Vignola c. 1552.

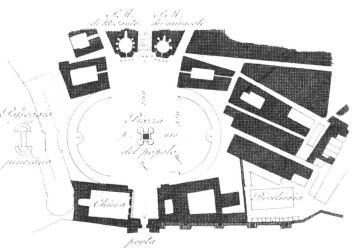

*S. M.
di M. Santo*   *S. M.
dei miracoli*

*Passeggio
pinciano*

*Piazza
del popolo*

Chiesa

Beccheria

porta

Porta Flaminia
ò del Popolo
1561

3

M. Bonarroti   Esterno   Interno   L. Bernini ec.
1655

Piazza del   Popolo

S. M. del popolo
ar. di Baccio Pintelli
1475

Palazzo
Capranica

Gesù e Maria al corso
ac. del Milanesi e Rainaldi
c. 1630.

S. Giacomo degl' incurabili
di Francesco da Volterra 1600.

4

5

S. Carlo al corso.
Onorio Lunghi ar. 1612.

Palaz. Ruspoli
B. Ammanati ar. c. 1530.

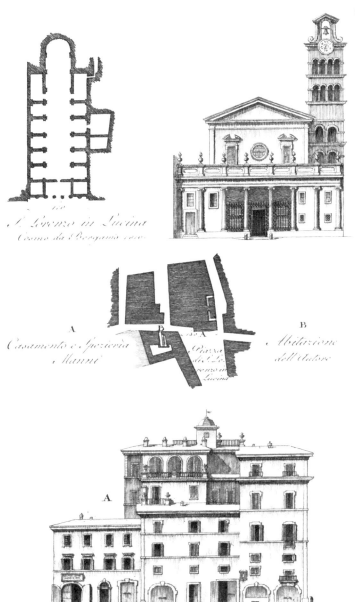

6

S. Lorenzo in Lucina
Cosmo da S.Bergamo ...

A
Casamento e Spezieria
Manni

B
Piazza
del S. Lo-
renzo in
Lucina

B
Abitazione
dell'Autore

A

Palazzo   Lozzana

Parti arch. 1834.

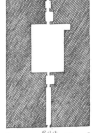

200

A Situaz. del fu
Arco di M. Aurelio

315.

Palazzo   Fiano

120

Palaz. Torlonia
Bracciano
Onorio Lunghi a
1575.

S. Silvestro in Capite
arch. di Gio. de Rossi. 1690.

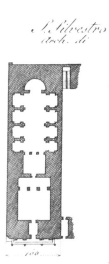

Casamento
Müller
Gio. Knapp 1835
arch.

Colonna Antonina e Palazzo Chigi
Giacomo della Porta
1660

Quartiere militare e Posta delle lettere

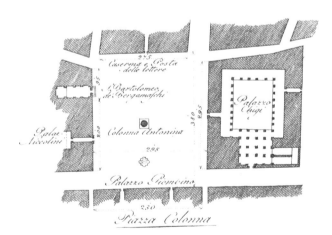

Palazzo Piombino

Piazza Colonna

Palazzo Niccolini
ar. di F. Paparelli

S. Bartolomeo dei Bergamaschi

C. de Dominicis

Palaz. Piombino
A. Servi rist. 1829.

Casa e Chiesa
dei Preti della Missione
ar. del P. della Torre 1741.

Ingresso

M. Citorio e Curia Innocenziana
Arch. del Bernini 1650.

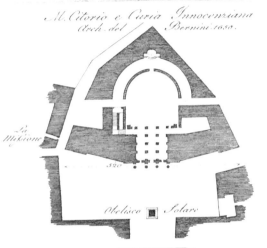

La
Missione

520

Obelisco Solare

Tempio d.° di Antonino — Dogana di terra — 1695.

250

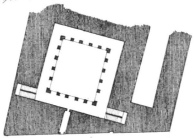

S. Ignazio.
Algardi 1685.

Collegio Romano. — B. Ammanati 1582.

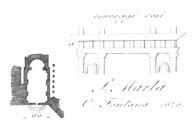

correggi così

S. Marta
C. Fontana   1570.

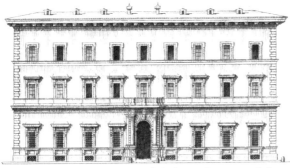

Palaz. Sciarra Colonna
di Flam. Ponzio
Portone di Sabaco c. 1603

S. Marcello
arch.
di Car. Fontana
16..

Palazzo Piombino
Arch. di Aleb Specchi c.1690.

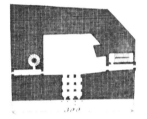

300

Palazzo Doria
Arch. di Valvasori c.1660.

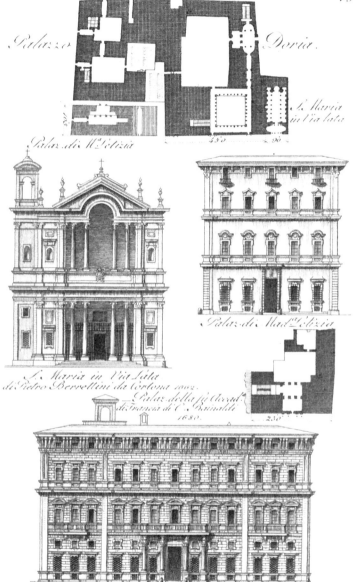

15

Palazzo   Doria.

S. Maria
in Via lata

Palaz: di: M.ª Letizia

Palaz: di: Mad.ª Letizia

S. Maria in Via Lata
di Pietro Berrettini da Cortona 1662.

Palaz: della fu Accad:
di Francia di C. Rainaldi
1680.

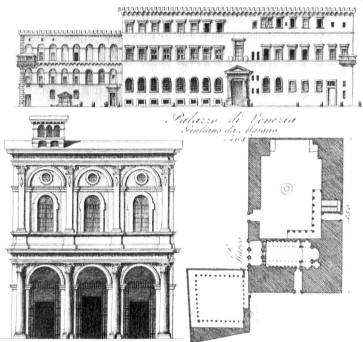

Palazzo di Venezia
Giuliano da Maiano
1468

S. Marco.

Sepolcro di C. Publ. Bibulo

Palaz. Torlonia
arch. del C.° Fontana
c. 1660

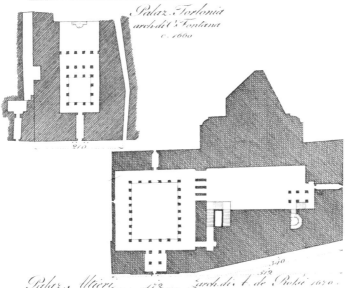

270

340
572

Palaz. Altieri 172 *arch. di A. de Rossi 1650.*

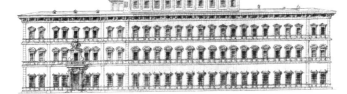

Palazzo Grazioli
di Camillo Arcucci
16..

210

Il Gesù
di Giac. della Porta
1575.

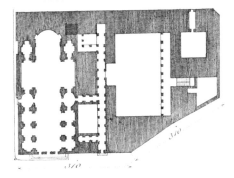

310

310

Palazzo Bolognetti
del Cav. Fuga c. 1735.

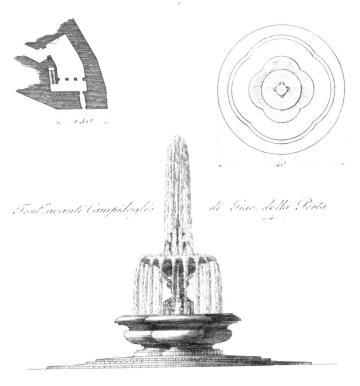

Font.ª avanti Campidoglio   *di Giac. della Porta*

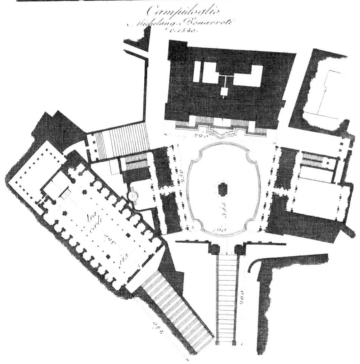

Campidoglio
Michelang. Bonarroti
c. 1540.

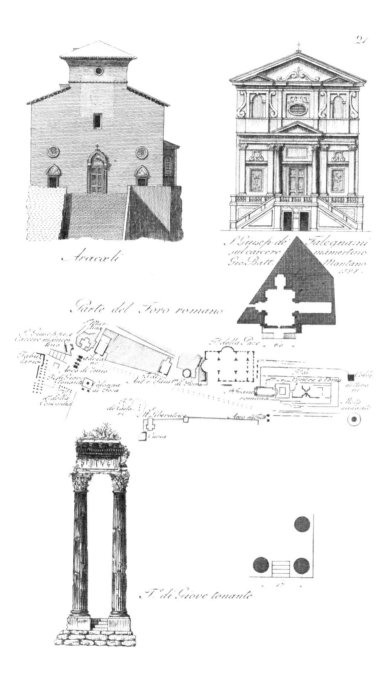

Aracœli

S.ᵗ Giusep. de' Falegnami
sul carcere mamertino
Gio. Batt.ᵗᵃ Montano
1598

Parte del Foro romano

T. di Giove tonante

Tempio della Concordia

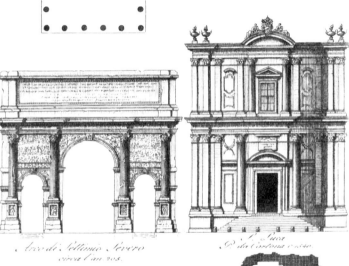

Arco de Settimio Severo
circa l'an 205.

S. Luca
P. da Cortona c. 1550.

S. Adriano

Col.ª di Foca

S. M. Liberatrice
Onorio Lunghi
1615.

Col. del T. di Castore e Polluce

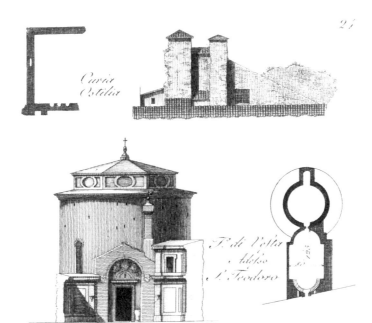

Curia
Ostilia

T.° di Vesta
adesso
S. Teodoro

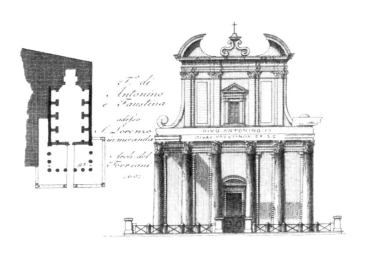

T.° di
Antonino
e Faustina
adesso
S. Lorenzo
in miranda
Arch. del
Torriani
1602

DIVO ANTONINO ET
DIVAE FAVSTINAE EX S C

SS. Cosmo e Damiano

Oratorio della Via Crucis

Tempio di Romolo e Remo

Tempio d. della Pace

Ingresso negli Orti Farnesiani del Vignola

S. Francesca Romana
C. Lombardi 1615.

Tempi di Venere e Roma

Arco di Tito ristaurato
da G. Valadier 1823.

Coloseo di Nerone

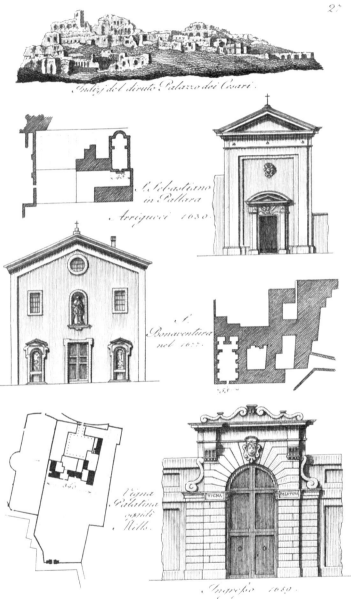

Indizj del diruto Palazzo dei Cesari.

S. Sebastiano
in Pallara
Arriguci 1630.

S.
Bonaventura
nel 1675.

Vigna
Palatina
appali
Mills.

Ingresso 1680.

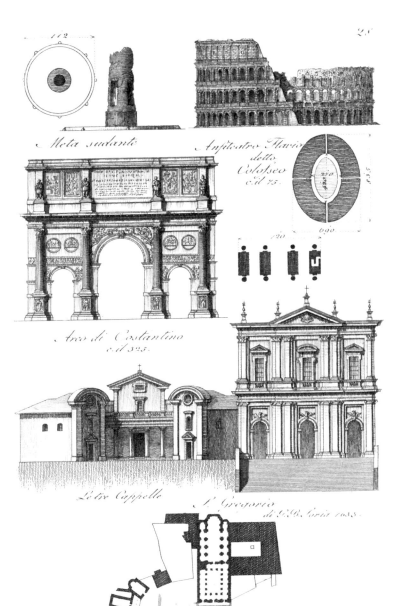

Meta sudante

Anfiteatro Flavio detto Colosseo c. d. 75.

Arco di Costantino c. d. 323.

Le tre Cappelle

S. Gregorio di G. B. Soria 1633.

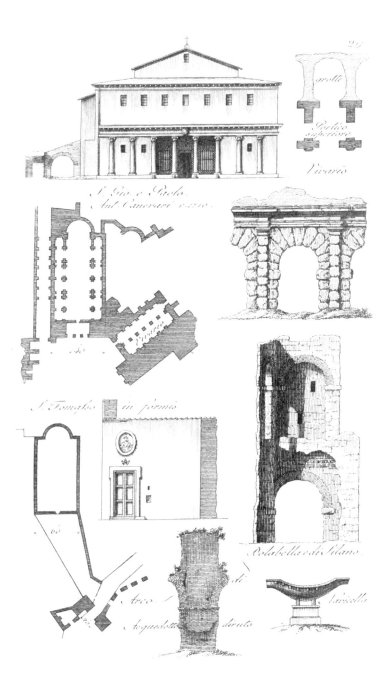

grotte

Portico superiore

Vivario

S. Gio. e Paolo.
Ant. Canovari vario.

Vivario

S. Tomaso in formis

Dolabella di Silano.

Arco

Acquedotto diruto

Lavicella

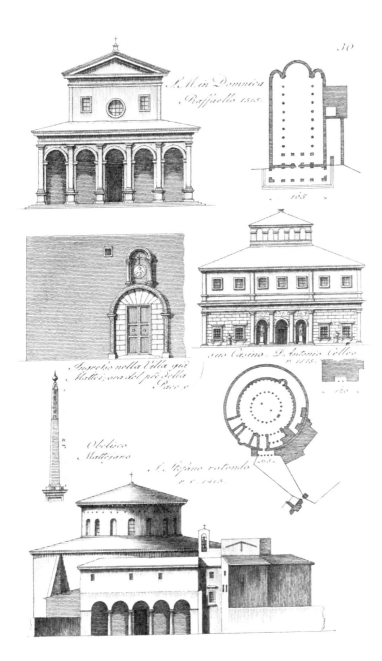

30

S. M. in Domnica
Raffaello 1513.

Ingresso nella Villa già
Mattei, ora del pr.e della
Pace o

Sno Casino. D'Antonio Celles
v. 1813.

Obelisco
Mattejano

S. Stefano rotondo
v. c. 1413.

SS. Quattro
rist.^e circa 1633.

Ospizio Lauretano

S. Clemente
n. c. 1715.

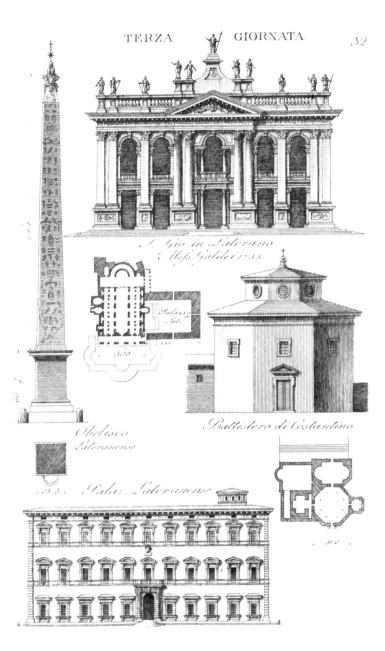

S. Gio in Laterano
Arch. Galilei 1735.

Obelisco
Lateranense

Battistero di Costantino

1586. Palaz. Lateranense

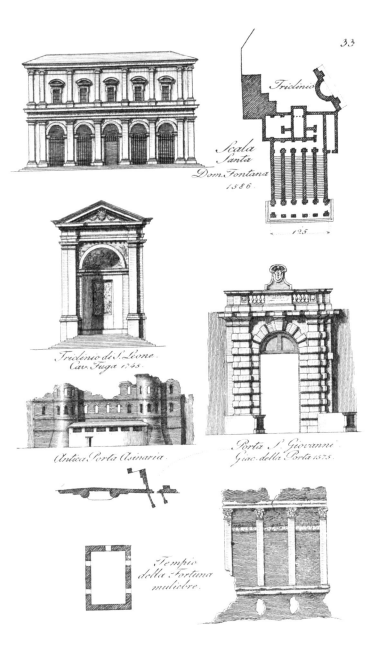

33

Scala
Santa
Dom. Fontana
1586.

Triclinio

125

Triclinio di S. Leone.
Cav. Fuga 1745.

Antica Porta Asinaria.

Porta S. Giovanni.
Giac. della Porta 1575.

Tempio
della Fortuna
muliebre.

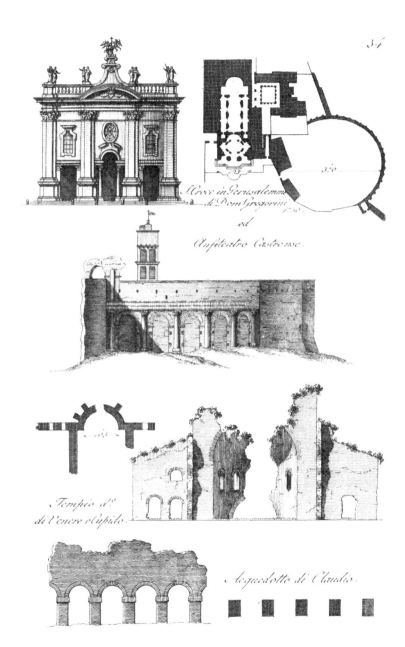

S.ᵗᵃ Croce in Gerusalemme
di Dom Gregorini 1730:
ed
Anfiteatro Castrense.

Tempio d.°
di Venere e Cupido.

Acquedotto di Claudio.

Porta Maggiore.

T.º d.º della Fortuna, e della Quiete.

Mausoleo di S. Elena d.º Tor Pignattara.

T.º d.º di Minerva Medica.

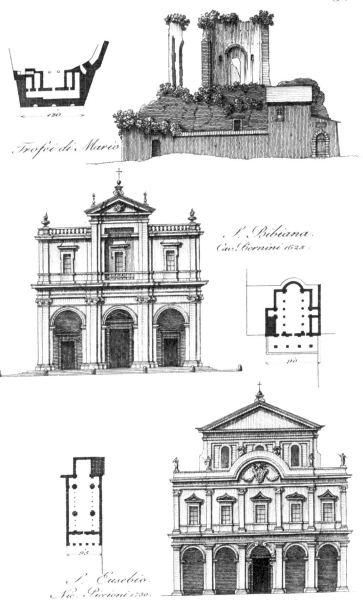

Trofei di Mario

S. Bibiana.
Cav. Bernini 1625.

S. Eusebio.
Nic. Piccioni 1750.

Porta S. Lorenzo.

Basilica di S. Lorenzo, nel 330. c.

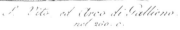

*S. Vito ed Arco di Gallieno,
nel 260. c.*

S. Antonio Abate. 1259.

38

Colon. eretta da Clem. VIII in memoria dell' absoluz. data ad Enrico IV re di Francia

120

Basilica di S. M. Maggiore
Ferd. Fuga c. 1750.

Colonna

360

Obelisco

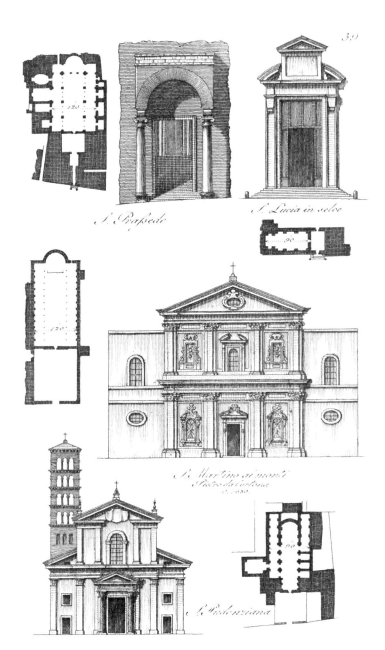

S. Prassede

S. Lucia in selce

S. Martino ai monti
Pietro da Cortona
c. 1650

S. Pudenziana

Bambin Gesù.
Ferd Fuga c 1760.

S. Pietro in vincoli.
F. Fontana 1705.

S. Francesco di Paola.
Luigi Bertoloni 1730.

Sette sale.

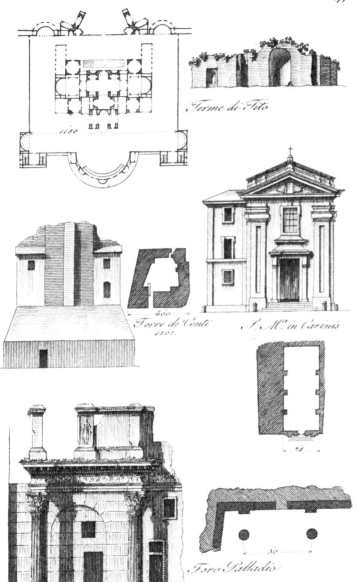

Terme di Tito

Torre de' Conti
1207.

S. M.ª in Carinis

Foro Palladio

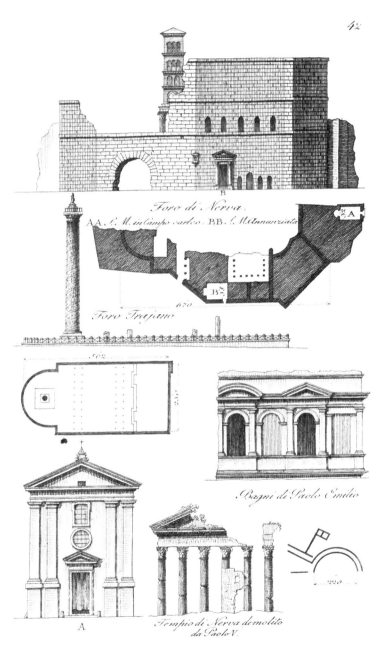

Foro di Nerva.

AA. S. M. in Campo carleo. BB. S. M. Annunziata.

Foro Trajano.

Bagni di Paolo Emilio

A.

Tempio di Nerva demolito
da Paolo V.

S. Maria   di Loreto
A. Sangallo   1510.

90

Il Nome di Ma
Mr. Derizet
1728.

140

A
A.A
SS. Apostoli

B
Palaz. Colonna
1420.

A
190

B

170

Palaz. Colonna

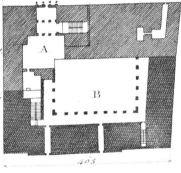

A

Palaz. già dell'
Accademia
di Francia.

Per il Prospetto
v. pag. 15.

B,B

Palazzo
Odescalchi

S. Croce dei Lucchesi
Mattia de Rossi
1650.

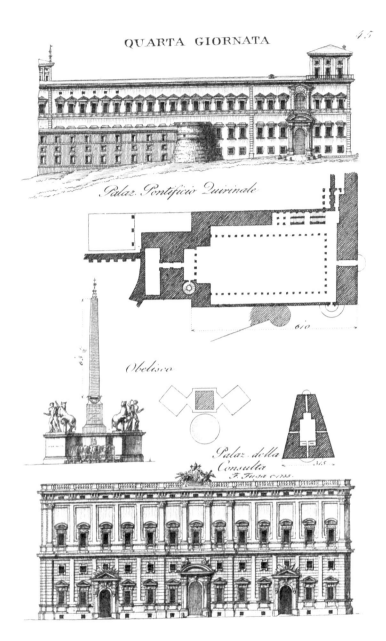

Palaz. Pontificio Quirinale

Obelisco

Palaz. della Consulta
F. Fuga c.1755.

Palaz. Rospigliosi

S. Silvestro   a M. Cavallo

560

80

S. Domenico e Sisto.
Vincenzo della Greca
c. 1630

Porta della Villa Aldobrandini

55

80

Torre d.^{le} delle Milizie

Sta Caterina a m. magnanapoli G. B. Soria 1563.

S. Bernardino

S. Agata

S. Vitale

S. Lorenzo
in Panxperna.
1575.

S. Maria
della sanità

S. Paolo
1º Eremita
Clemente Orlandi

S.
Dionigi
1619.

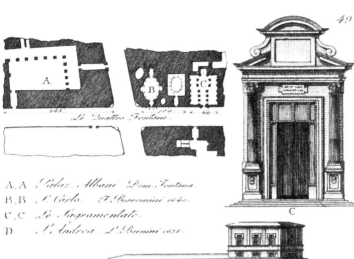

Le Quattro Fontane.

A, A *Palaz. Albani . Dom. Fontana .*
B, B *S. Carlo . F. Borromini 1640 .*
C, C *Le Sagramentate .*
D   *S. Andrea . L. Bernini 1678 .*

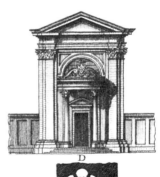

C

A

B

D

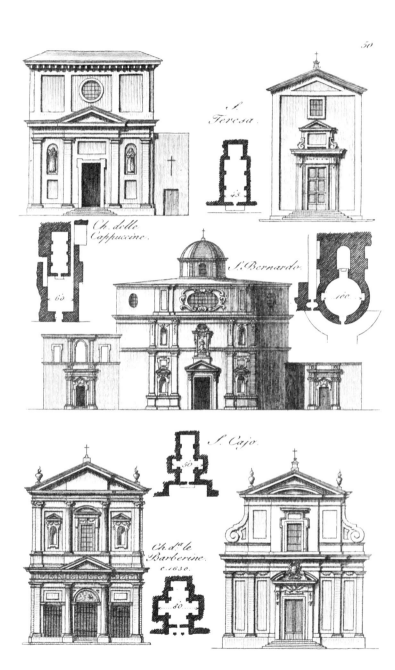

50

S. Teresa.

Ch. delle Cappuccine.

S. Bernardo.

S. Cajo.

Ch.da le Barberine. c.1650.

51

S. Susanna.
Carlo Maderno. 1603.

Fonte dell'Acqua Felice.
Dom. Fontana 1583.

Terme Diocleziane.

S. M.ᵃ della
Vittoria.
G.ᵗᵗ Batt.
Soria
1600.

60

65

10

860

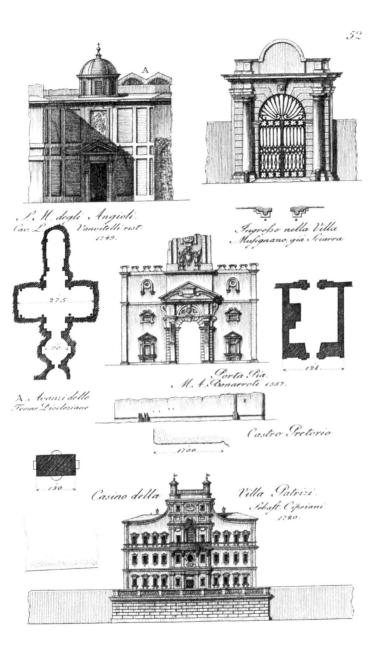

S. M. degli Angioli.
Cav. L. Vanvitelli rist.
1749.

Ingresso nella Villa
Musignano, già Sciarra

27.5

20

Porta Pia.
M. A. Bonarroti 1557.

A. Avanzi delle
Terme Diocleziane

Castro Pretorio

1700

150

Casino della

Villa Patrizi.
Sebast. Cipriani
1720.

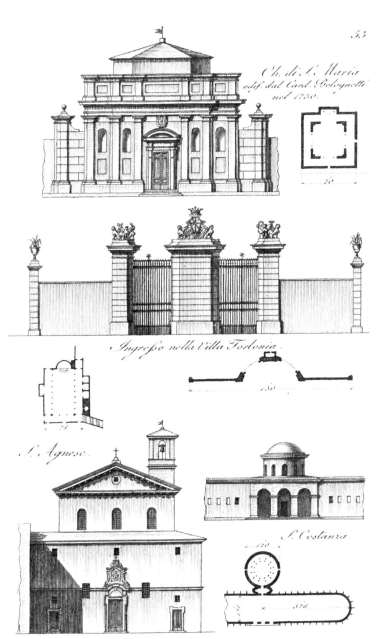

Ch. di S. Maria edif. dal Card. Bolognetti nel 1750.

10

Ingresso nella Villa Torlonia.

130

75

S. Agnese.

S. Costanza.

170

376

Ponte Nomentano.

Porta Salara.

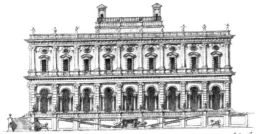

– 90. –

90

Casino della Villa Albani — Card. Aless. Albani dis. 1760.

Ponte Salaro

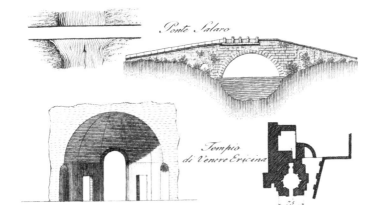

Tempio di Venere Ericina

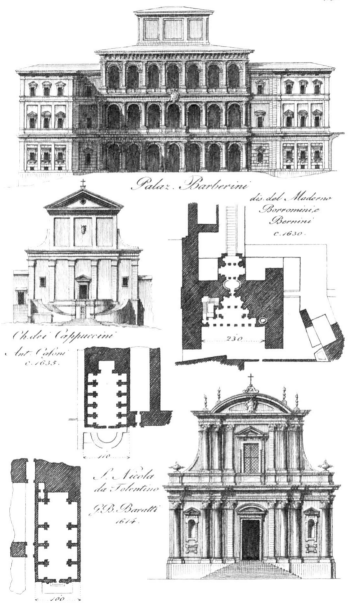

Palaz. Barberini

dis. del Maderno
Borromini, e
Bernini
c.1630.

230

Ch. dei Cappuccini
Ant. Casoni
c.1635.

110

S. Nicola
da Tolentino
G.B. Baratti
1614.

100

24

Ingresso in Villa
Ludovisi

Fontane nella
Piazza Barberini

dis. del cav. Bernini

Tritone

S. Isidoro.

Ant. Casoni 1622.

63

Fontana di Trevi . Nicola Salvi 1735.

S. Vincenzo ed Anastasio .
Martino Lunghi
1650.

S. Mª in Trivio .
Giac. del Duca .
1660 .

Acquedotto dell'acqua Vergine .
rist . da Claudio imp .

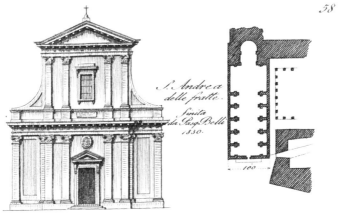

S.ᵗᵉ Andrea
delle fratte.
finita
da Pasq:Belli
1830.

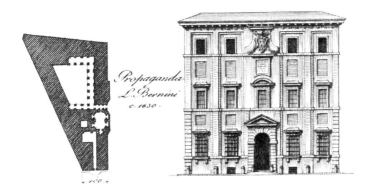

Propaganda
L. Bernini
c. 1630.

Palaz: di Spagna
Ant: Celles rist.ᵗᵒ
1815.

59

Palaz. Mignanelli

Locanda d.ᵃ la grand'Europa

AA. *Trinità dei Monti.*
B.B *Obelisco Sallustiano.*
C.C *Fontana detta*
     la barcaccia.

Scalinata
in piazza di
Spagna.

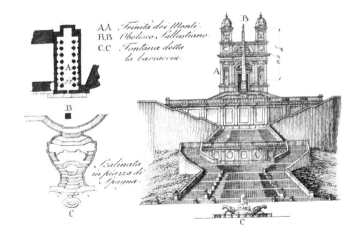

Accad.ᵃ di Francia   Annib.ᵉ Lippi c. 1550.

Ingresso in Villa Borghese.
Luigi Canina 1828.
c. 135

Muro
torto

Casamento
Stivani.
Enrico Calderari
rifᵗᵒ 1833.

di giunta
alla pag. 5.

Mausoleo di Augusto, adibito Anfiteatro per ispettacoli

S. Rocco.
G. Valadier 1833.

S. Girolamo de' Schiavoni
Mart. Lunghi e Fontana c. 1590.

Porto di Ripetta.

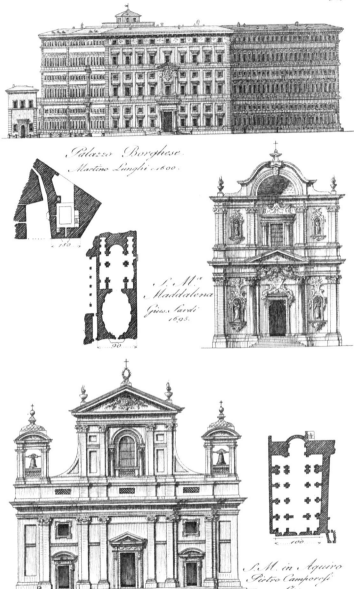

62

Palazzo Borghese.
Martino Lunghi. 1600.

S. M.ª Maddalena
Giuss. Sardi
1695.

S. M. in Aquiro
Pietro Camporesi
17.

Pantheon

250

Obelisco

63

100

Le Stimate.
Ant.º Canevari.
c. 1680.

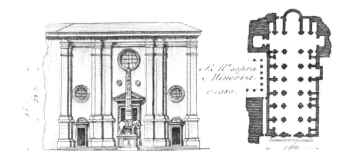

S.ª M.ª sopra
Minerva.
c. 1380.

100

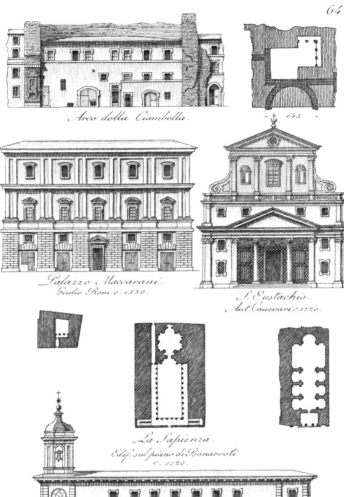

Arco della Ciambella.

145

Palazzo Maccarani.
Giulio Rom. c. 1530.

S. Eustachio.
Ant. Canevari c. 1720.

La Sapienza.
Edif. sul piano di Bonarroti
c. 1520.

Teatro Valle. — G. Valadier 1822.

Palaz. del Governo. — Paolo Marucelli 1600. c.

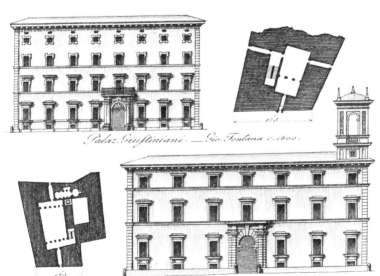

Palaz. Giustiniani. — Gio. Fontana c. 1600.

Palaz. Altemps — Baldassar. Peruzzi c. 1530.

S. Luigi dei Francesi.
Giac. della Porta
c. 1590.

S. Agostino.
Baccio Pintelli.
1483.

150

S. Apollinare.
Ferd. Fuga
c. 1750.

120

Palaz. Lancellotti.

Franc. da Volterra
c. 1630.

S. Antonio
dei Portughesi.
Mart. Lunghi c. 1695.

S. Salvatore in Lauro.
Ottavio Mascherini c. 1613.

Palaz. Cicciaporci
Giulio Rom. c. 1530.

Palaz. Niccolini
Giac. Sansovino c. 1540.

105

62

Casa di Raffaello.
Via dei Coronari N°.
124, 5

Banco di S. Spirito.

30

38

SS. Celso e Giuliano.
Carlo de Dominicis.
c. 1735.

85.

88.

Palaz.
Gabrielli.

336.

S. M.ᵃ in Vallicella.
Mart. Lunghi. c. 1575.

Oratorio.
F. Borromini. c. 1645.

Palaz. Sora.
creduto di Bramante
Lazari
1500

S. Mᵃ della Pace.
Pietro da Cortona
c.1660.

S. M. dell'Anima
Bramante
c.1500

A.A. S. Agnese F. Borromini c 1645.
B,B. Fontana con Obe- lisco L.Bernini
C. Palaz Pamfili c 1650
D. S. Vicola dei Lo- renesi
E,E. Palaz Bra- schica Morelli
c 1790.

A

B

Piazza Navona.

S. Pantaleo
Valadier 1806.

E

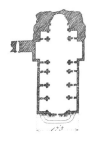

72

S. Andrea della Valle.
P. Olivieri c.1550.

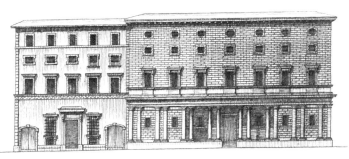

Palaz. Massimo.
Bald. Peruzzi c.1525.

Palaz. Pio. Cam. Arcucci
c.16..

A
S. M.
de grotta
pinta.

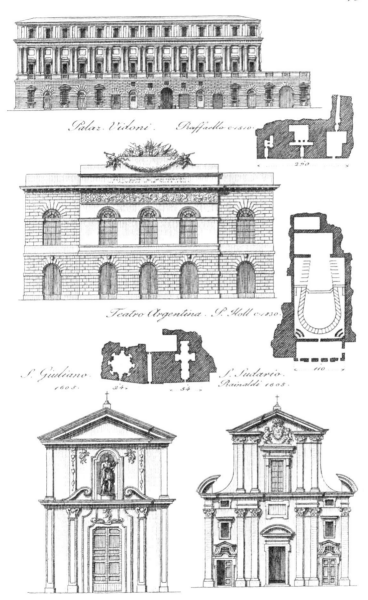

Palaz. Vidoni. Raffaello c. 1510.

Teatro Argentina. S. Holl c. 1830.

S. Giuliano. 1605. 24. 54. S. Sudario. Rainaldi 1605. 110. 250.

S. Elena
dei Credenzieri.

S. Nicola ai Cesarini;
ed AA avanzi di antico
Tempio.

S. Lucia e Palaz. Ginnasi

S. Stanislao
dei Pollacchi.

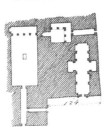

Palaz. Mattei A. C. Maderno
c. 1550.

S. M.ª in Campitelli. C. Rainaldi c. 1660.

S. Caterina dei Funari B.
Giac. della Porta
1564.

Portico di Ottavia,
e C. S. Angelo in Pescheria
1700.

Palaz. Orsini
edif: sulle rovine del Teatro di Marcello
da Bald. Peruzzi c. 1530.

S. Nicola in carcere.
Giac. della Porta 1593.

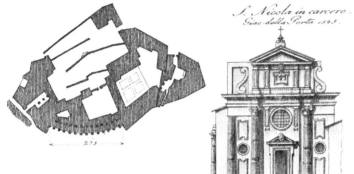

S. M.ª della Consolazione.
Pasq. Belli 1527.

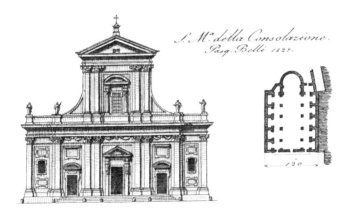

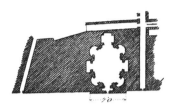

77

S.ª Galla.
c. 1660.

S. Eligio
dei ferrari
1563.

S. Giovanni decollato.
c. 1500.

Arco di Giano.

S. Giorgio in velabro .. A.A Arco degli Orefici

Cloaca maßima

S. Anastasia Luigi Arigucci c.1630.

Area del Circo maßimo, oggidi orti.

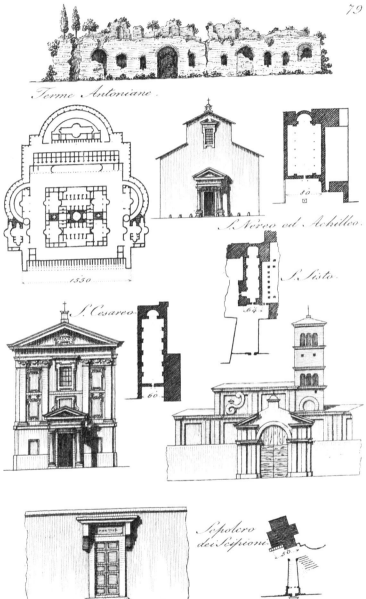

Terme Antoniane.

S. Nereo ed Achilleo.

S. Sisto.

S. Cesareo.

Sepolcro dei Scipioni.

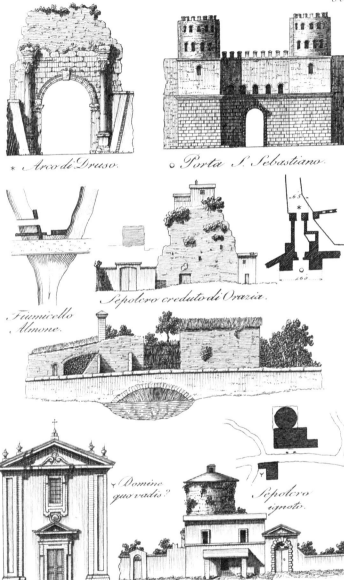

* *Arco di Druso.*   ○ *Porta S. Sebastiano.*

Sepolcro creduto di Orazia.

Fiumicello Almone.

Domine quo vadis?   *Sepolcro ignoto.*

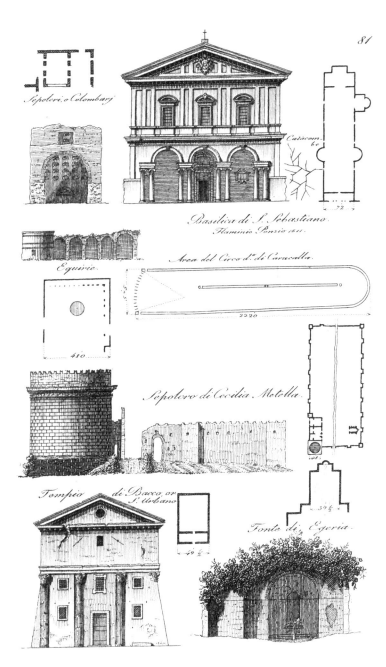

Sepolcri, o Colombarj

Catacombe

Basilica di S. Sebastiano.
Flaminio Ponzio 1611.

Area del Circo d.º di Caracalla.

E'quirie.

2220

480

Sepolcro di Cecilia Metella.

Tempio di Bacco, or S. Urbano.

Fonte di Egeria.

T.º del dio redicolo.

Porta S. Paolo

Piramide di C. Cestio *

Basilica di S. Paolo.

S. M.ª scala G.

Covli V'ignola c.1582.

210

Le 3. Chiese a S. Paolo alle tre fontane
S.S. Vincenzo ed Anastasio.

S. Paolo
Giac. della Porta
1590.

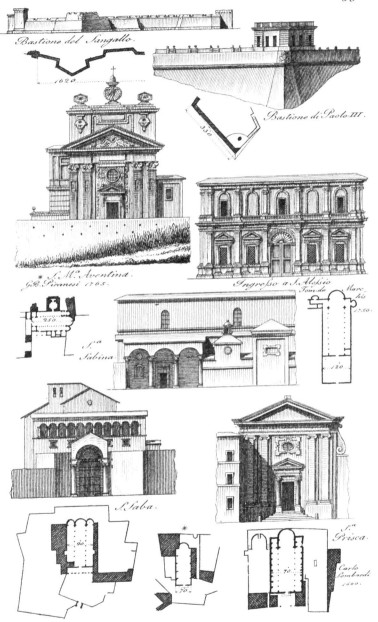

83

Bastione del Sangallo.

1620.

Bastione di Paolo III.

330

* S. M.ª Aventina.
G.B. Piranesi 1765.

Ingresso a S. Alessio

S.ª Sabina

250

Marc.
his
1750.

120

S. Saba.

S.ª Prisca.

Carlo
Lombardi
1600.

90

70

70

84

S. Anna dei Calzettari

Arco d.º di Orazio Coclite.

Tempio di Vesta.

S. M.ª in Cosmedin. Gius. Sardi 1718.

T.º della Fortuna Virile.

Casa di Cola di Rienzo.

Ponte rotto

S. Salvatore.

S.ª Balbina.

Ponte Cestio e Ponte Fabricio

S. Bartolommeo
M. Lunghi

S. Gio. Colabita
1600

S. M.ª dell'Orto
M. Lunghi

Ripa grande ed Ospizio di S. Michele
Mattia de Rossi 1600

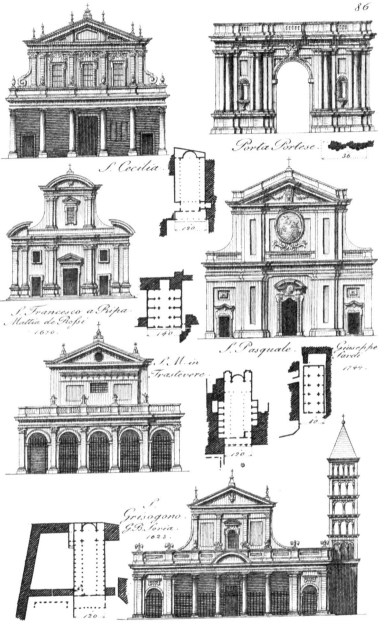

86

S. Cecilia.

Porta Portese.
36.

S. Francesco a Ripa.
Mattia de Rossi.
1670.

S. Pasquale.
Giuseppe Sardi.
1744.

S. M. in Trastevere.

S. Grisogono.
G. B. Soria.
1623.

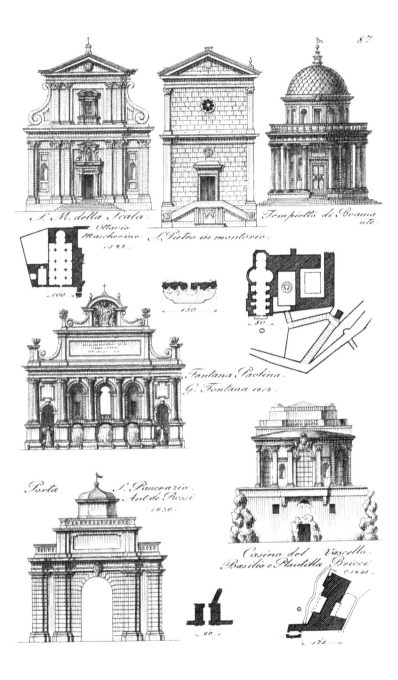

S.ᵗᵃ M. della Scala.
Ottavio
Mascherino
1592.

S.ᵗ Pietro in montorio.

Tempietto di Brama
nte.

Fontana Paolina.
G. Fontana 1612.

Porta S. Pancrazio.
Ant. de Rossi
1630.

Casino del Vascello.
Basilio e Plautilla Bricci.
c.1640.

Ingresso nella Villa
Panfili Doria
Aless. Algardi
c. 1645.

Casino Corsini. Simone Salvi
c. 1725.

S. Pancrazio.

130

123.

Porta
Settimiana.

20

650

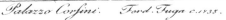

Palazzo Corsini. Ferd. Fuga c. 1735.

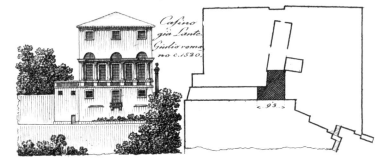

Casino
già Lante.
Giulia roma
no c. 1520.

93

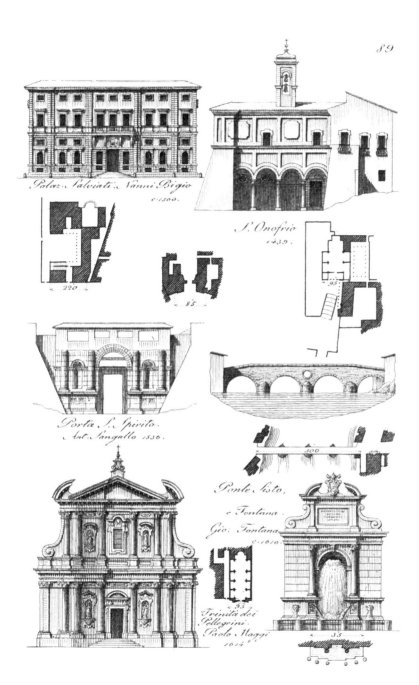

89

Palaz. Salviati. Nanni Bigio
c. 1500.

S. Onofrio
1439.

220

85

Porta S. Spirito.
Ant. Sangallo 1536.

500

Ponte Sisto,
e Fontana.
Gio. Fontana
c. 1610.

95

Trinità dei
Pellegrini.
Paolo Maggi
1614

35

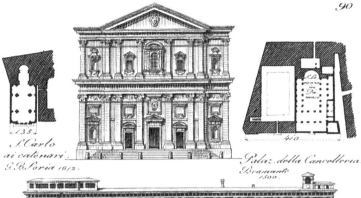

S. Carlo
ai catenari.
G.B.Soria 1612.

Palaz. della Cancelleria.
Bramante
1500.

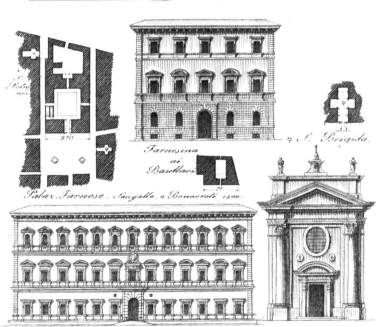

Palaz. Farnese. Sangallo e Bonarroti 1500.

Farnesina
ai
Baullari.

S. Brigida.

Ingresso nella villa Massimo.
(di quinta alla)
45. pag. 51.

Palaz. Spada.
Giulio Mazzoni
1540.

S. M.ª della morte.
Cav. Fuga
1737.

250.

Palazzo
Falconieri +

80. 350.

55.
S. Caterina
della ruota.

S. Girolamo della carità. Dom. Castelli
1660.

Carceri
nuove.

58.

170.

S. Caterina ✝ dei Sanesi.
Paolo Posi
1770.

S. Spirito
dei
Napole
tani

Palaz Ricci

Nanni
di Bac-
cio bigio

S. Biagio

S. Eligio degli Ore-
fici.

S. Filip Neri.

S. Anna dei Bresciani.   S. Niccolò
Vescovo

S. M. del Suffragio. C. Rainaldi 1675.

Confraternita del Gonfalone

.58.

Palaz. Sacchetti
Ant. Sangallo c.1535.

265

Farnesina alla lungara
Baldaf. Peruzzi
c.1520.

165

S. Gio. dei Fiorentini
Alef. Galilei
c.1723.

180

Palazzo di Firenze. *Vignola 1550.*

150

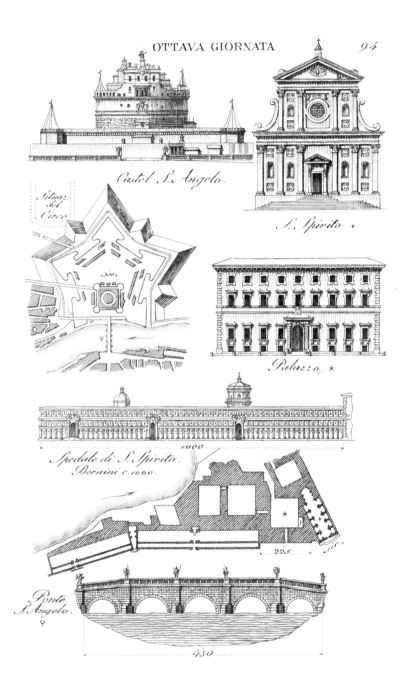

Castel S. Angelo.

S. Spirito.

Situaz. del Circo

Palazzo.

Spedale di S. Spirito.
Bornini c. 1660.

1000

225

Ponte
S. Angelo.

430

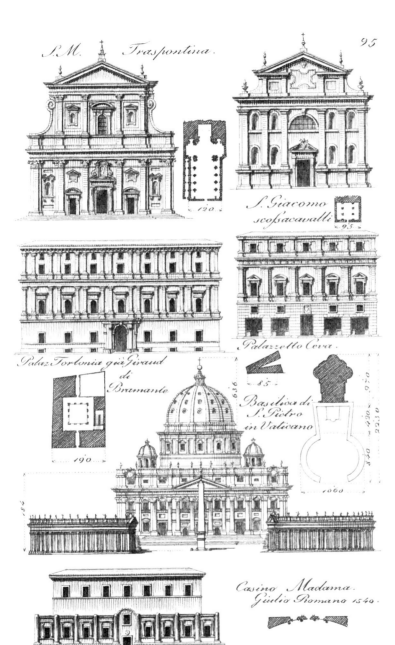

95

S.M. Traspontina.

S. Giacomo scossacavalli.
‹ 120. › ‹ 95. ›

Palazzetto Cova.

Palaz. Torlonia già Giraud di Bramante
‹ 85. › ‹ 190. ›

Basilica di S. Pietro in Valicano
‹ 1000. ›

Casino Madama.
Giulio Romano 1540.

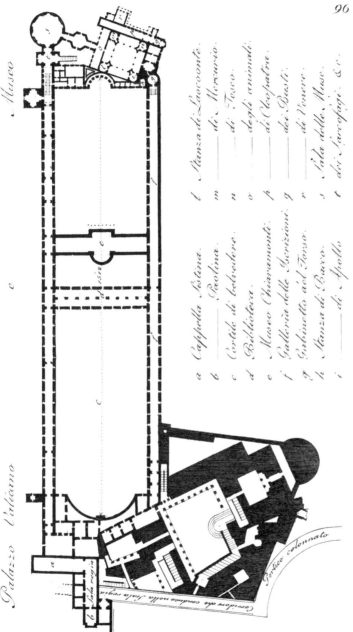

Palazzo Vaticano

Museo

a Cappella Sistina.
b —— Paolina.
c Cortile di belvedere.
d Biblioteca.
e Museo Chiaramonte.
f Galleria delle Iscrizioni.
g Gabinetto del Torso.
h Stanza di Bacco.
i —— di Apollo.

l Stanza di Laocoonte.
m —— di Mercurio.
n —— di Teseo.
o —— degli animali.
p —— di Cleopatra.
q —— dei Busti.
r —— di Venere.
s Sala delle Muse.
t —— dei Sarcofagi. &c.

Portico colonnato

Corridore che conduce nella Sala regia

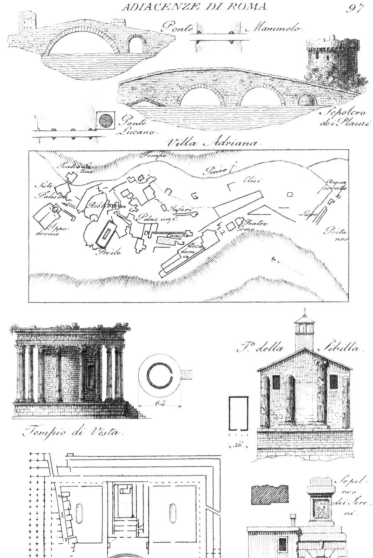

Ponte Mammolo.

Sepolcro dei Plauzi

Ponte Lucano.

Villa Adriana.

Tempio di Vesta.

T.° della Sibilla.

Villa di Mecenate.

Sepolcro dei Sereni.

Villa di Mecenate.

430

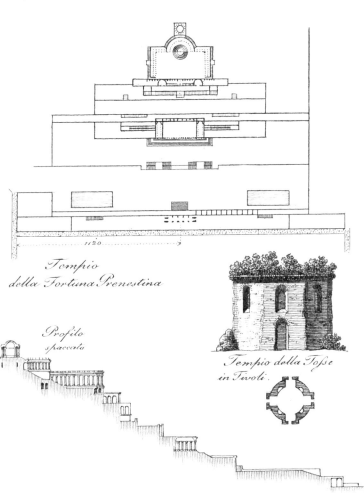

*Tempio
della Fortuna Prenestina*

1120

*Profilo
spaccato*

*Tempio della Tosse
in Tivoli.*

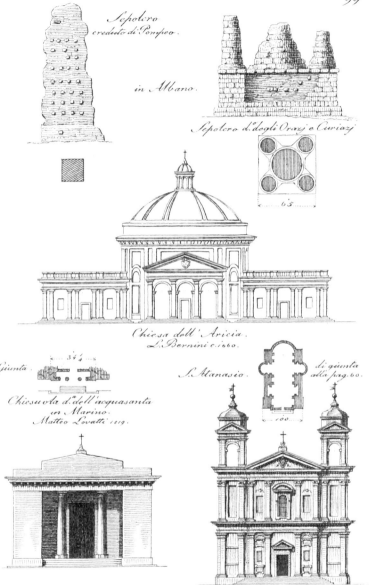

Sepolcro
creduto di Pompeo.

in Albano.

Sepolcro d.º degli Orazj e Curiazj.

Chiesa dell'Aricia.
L. Bernini c. 1660.

Giunta.

Chiesuola d.ª dell'acquasanta
in Marino.
Matteo Lovatti 1819.

S. Atanasio.

di giunta
alla pag. 60.